Infinite Altars

poems

Infinite Altars

JAMES BRASFIELD

Louisiana State University Press   Baton Rouge

Published by Louisiana State University Press
Copyright © 2016 by James Brasfield
All rights reserved
Manufactured in the United States of America
LSU Press Paperback Original
First printing

Designer: Barbara Neely Bourgoyne
Typeface: Livory
Printer and binder: LSI

Grateful acknowledgment is made to the following magazines, in which many of these poems first appeared: *Black Warrior Review, Disquieting Muses Quarterly Review, Grist, Heliotrope, Imported Breads: Literature of Cultural Exchange* (anthology), *Kestrel, Miramar, New Orleans Review, Petroglyph, The Pinch, Poetry International, Poets.org: The Academy of American Poets Poem-a-Day Series, Shenandoah, Southern Humanities Review, Southern Poetry Review, The Southern Review, Stand, Tar River Poetry, Valparaiso Poetry Review,* and the *Worcester Review.*

"Early Afternoon, Having Just Left the Chapel of San Francesco" appeared in *Feathers from the Angel's Wing: Poems Inspired by the Paintings of Piero della Francesca,* edited by Dana Prescott (Persea Books, 2016).

Special thanks especially to my wife Charlotte Holmes, and to Robin Becker, John Bensko, Kathryn Stripling Byer, W. S. Di Piero, and Carl Little for their help in preparing this collection.

Library of Congress Cataloging-in-Publication Data
Names: Brasfield, James, author.
Title: Infinite altars : poems / James Brasfield.
Description: Baton Rouge : Louisiana State University Press, [2016]
Identifiers: LCCN 2016008117 | ISBN 978-0-8071-6424-2 (softcover : acid-free paper) | ISBN 978-0-8071-6425-9 (pdf) | ISBN 978-0-8071-6426-6 (epub) | ISBN 978-0-8071-6427-3 (mobi)
Classification: LCC PS3552.R32755 A6 2016 | DDC 811/.54—dc23 LC record available at http://lccn.loc.gov/2016008117

The paper in this book meets the guidelines for permanence and durability of the Committee on Production Guidelines for Book Longevity of the Council on Library Resources. ∞

In memory of Oleh Lysheha

Contents

PART I

Northern Bay 3
Early Afternoon, Having Just Left the
 Chapel of San Francesco 4
Homage to Piero della Francesca 6
Window Frame 8
Expleasure 10
Cézanne 11
The Magic Gardener 13
Map 15
Clemency 17
The Night of Daydream 20
Only to Listen 27
Carmine Street 28

PART II

Brooklyn to Menatay 33
Shore and Sea 34
Acqua Alta 35
The Entrepreneur 36
Sequel 38
The Incorporation 40
Tributary 42
Ritsos 44
Coming Down 45

Turning Fifty, Mid April 46
Standard Time 47
Afternoons into Evenings 48

PART III
The Renaissance 59
Islanders 60
Demopolis 64
Strange Coming Near 65
Stray Stone 66
Daylight Ghosts 67
Soundings 68
Summer Solstice 73
Kierkegaard Returns to a Patch of Partridgeberry 75
The Visit 77
Sweet Madness of Song 78
The Song of the Eastern Meadowlark 79

Notes 81

PART I

NORTHERN BAY
for Jen and Pat

Perhaps someone at the lake remembers
the wind, as it is here, through the trees:
May, dandelions, dew laden, open
in the meadow, seeds aloft, and already
a poplar, leafed out, bears its summer shape,
its moment of clouds' wind-carved symmetry
in the branches, a yellow warbler
come and gone in its moment of light.

The sun sets through rain-slacked clouds,
its sheen bristling on the current
crossing the bay, brightening tide pools,
their veils inching out, lapping mud,
and sundown backlit, as on another day
here, for someone else—the heron
scales in, settling himself on his long legs
steady on smoothed stones.

Diamond glints coming in, wind-driven,
a rhythm like rows of woodgrain
through a plank table, such insistence lapping
stones, their stillness below what passes . . .
each stone its sudden luminous streak of rain,
as if etched on a blank window, a room
arrayed with what's been salvaged from a tide:
what a hand reached for, what remains.

EARLY AFTERNOON, HAVING JUST LEFT THE CHAPEL OF SAN FRANCESCO
for my son Will

Radiant the delayed calmness,
—Do you feel it, I said.—Yes, you said,

of what only each can know,
kernel of radiance, the *globo terrestre*

of a water drop, not the passing adaptations
of canonical light, but seconds stilled—

our hearts beating through the moments—centuries
of the next tick of a watch relieved,

a world enough in time to imagine
Piero walk to work across cobblestones

toward a completion, his close attention
to sunlight passing through shadows

owned by the sharp angles of buildings,
sunrays warming what they touch.

Piero, first a painter, is not a monk.
He will make what welcomes light

a source of light: slow the day
he will add lucent black wings

to white feathers of the magpie
ever alight on a roof-edge.

I found a feather on a stone, feather I thought
from the angel's wing, that arc of light

held aloft in descent, shared with us
and Constantine in his dream.

I think of a white egret returning home near
the high creek, through unwavering

evening light, to sleep, sleep at Sansepolcro,
where we were headed in a rental car.

HOMAGE TO PIERO DELLA FRANCESCA

> Drawing we understand as meaning outlines and contours contained in things. Proportion we say is these outlines and contours positioned in proportion in their places. Coloring we mean as giving the colors as they are shown in the things, light and dark according as the light makes them vary.
>
> —PIERO DELLA FRANCESCA, *De prospectiva pingendi*

If in the midst of the ever ongoing,
no matter the forms of violence and our fear,
if we find rest, the presence of shadows and light
harbors the tranquil moment. From our
seeing more closely, always more closely
in our extreme attention, light's angles and subtle shade,
a recognition comes, this for the first time always—
such presence, hidden from plain sight, emerges,
as though it trusted our seeing—the old, ladderback chair
in sunlight, shadowed under the open window, new
in an old way, a new orientation
in an insulate calm.

Something of that calmness goes with us
back into the world, an intimate vista
deepening a third dimension when we turn away,
and perhaps what we call the inner life is
such intimacies: a then, and a now,
and a now to come, to enter into what comes to us,
depicted always in forms of light,
the revelation found
as if it had always been waiting,
and always a surprise, the separation from time—
an egg's shadow on the kitchen counter
at noon passing, shifting the appearance of the egg,
and we feel what we see. How simply
we enter that feeling—if only
for a little while, inseparable from what we see,

not knowing we were on a journey,
a silent drama underway, fleshed out, leading us
further into the world. The kitchen
and no one there—morning shadows and stillness
and birdsong and sounds of traffic
passing through the open window, and yet
a stillness, like no other, inhabits the room.

Outside, the morning mist capping the mountains
recedes farther than you would have ever thought
possible in late morning light, the mountains closer
in their clarity, the miles of the range in deep perspective,
in infinite variations of light—
how the oak, close by, changes,
instant by instant, slowly, at the speed of light.

We close our eyes and hold the image:
the chair at the foot of the mountains—
the egg our silent moment of joy
at noon, each instant

its pyramid within a cube.

WINDOW FRAME

A validation of light
is as far as I can see, as far
as time allows outside the window:

poplar, inlet, river, and far shore—
its trees and mountains. Panel, wall,
canvas, or paper, each its possibility

for pulse to make what will not change
when light passes, a perspective
measured in measured space,

not a photographic record of time
but light spreading outward
from the nerves. Framed by the window,

branches of the leaning poplar
grow longer and higher on one side.
Dark clouds at dusk fill in among the leaves.

Halfway, up the other side of the tree
lies a wide plane of wooded hills—
the orange sun dissolves through clouds

above the ridgelines. All I see out there
is passing through poplar leaves,
as light passes here—breath and pulse.

The longer I watch the tree at nightfall,
the more I understand the view in relation.
Yesterday at the window is circumscribed:

the places I've been keep their vanishing points . . .
morning's soft glare on the fountain sparkling,
brightening—translucent shadows

recede over the Tuscan piazza,
a sparrow, its moment there, poised
at the rim of the fountain, recalled

long after I've turned away. Now to find
the bird in the master's painting, from a time
long before I existed—bird at a fountain,

the light sensate, the transference
a conjuration of such a small pulse
from out there, emanating its soft glare,

not from a mirror, but light's calm motions
from the panel, and the sparrow
from that time on. . . . At the window,

a leaf-stem's sudden release,
a sound to imagine—
the leaf touching summer grass.

EXPLEASURE

    How time slowed when any thought
or apprehension of the next instant
        vanished (no obligation, then or later),

    how in that long moment, all at once,
yet without surprise, how what was close
        was present in a sudden suspense,

    as such things rarely exist
as they did then, each apart from all,
        seen as it might be truly,

    and gave way to a pleasure
that had long been missing,
        to *expleasure,* as if I were akin

    to the smallest things—ribs
of a leaf, penny on a dresser—
        of a saving stillness, doubtless

    always here, just beyond
the scrim of what calls us
        from that silent astonishment,

    the more so since the feeling
dissolves with its presence of detail
        merging with a distant seeing,

    as when I walk through a room
and nothing is equal there to the calm
        from the simply seen.

CÉZANNE

Each step a penultimate moment,
an absence opening toward sunlight
through scrub oak in late morning mist:
the least bit here, a little more
in the passing into. He says, *Let it be seen
clearly through the smoke of the place*—
a now to then, patched in as he sees it,
presence a vantage point,
vantage point a presence,
where shadows at noon or night are cast.

Toward the forest and granite quarry—
tall grass and boulders, alive
as facets of a river, lead across a meadow.
What is seen is changed at a pine
at a grove of poplars, where foothills begin
their luminous shade, their rhythms of bearing,
no matter the stillness of acquisition
parceled by light imparting wholeness
upon the making—a motif conjuring
boundaries for a forest, its quarry.

In the mountains where stones lie uncollected
and the blackcap sings unafraid
in these endless provinces, the master,
as if to lift a final rail through the first post,
plies a measure toward a last emptiness
to be transformed, an inherent
abstraction of place, and thinks
*When the last oscillation of stillness
is complete, I'll move on between
the tensions, mapped out and filled in.*

At the Chateau Noir, the orange house
stares from a slope of trees. Occupied,

he bends a little left or right,
completing the balance,
then climbs to a plateau for the vista
and close surroundings, to rescue
again a then from now, to compose,
as from the smell of fields, sensations,
tones built up and pieced together,
an atmosphere for his animate province.

Each time he adds the never before,
a forked pine perhaps to his ritual terrain,
and standing at dusk holding the bird's late trill
and high note stretched before the last,
he thumbs a pebble in his palm.

THE MAGIC GARDENER
in memory of Stanley Kunitz

1. Seminar

Knowing deep in the self
was a plot to dig,
you searched the ceiling
often as you addressed us,
as if you plied
with judgmental hand
the philosopher's stone
to let the dormant sprout,
to cultivate
the slow transmutation—
the annual become
the new perennial.
Raised by the earth's tilt
weeds come randomly,
yet the violets at your window
or in your garden thrive
by your tacit motto: Care
how each bloom comes to be,
each opening to the other,
the wildflower to share
the ground beside the rose.

2. Final Class

A spring night at your Village apartment . . .
        Fatherless late-bloomer, voluntary
    taken hold, you dealt cards from the Tarot.

For each you gave the interpretation:
        mine, discouraging, but I still believe
    your intent was more than diversion.

When you saw me uprooted, divulged
        by drawn luck, you planted the antidote,
    "You must change your life."

I did and am *on the edge of the road*,
        remembering always now your words
    the sands whispered and *stones taught*.

I follow the cowpath where you pointed
        up the steep, impossible slope
    where blossoms defy winter.

MAP

From trees a bird song, from tall reeds
a man standing in an oak skiff,
not yet yours, crosses the river—
morning mist on the smooth current
unfolding a map of autumnal shadows—earth
turning eastward, no matter the stillness.

Scattered high, ravens turn back
over beet fields. Wind shoves
gently the shoulders of the man
edging the oar patiently. Ripples
around the oar and the skiff's wake
spread, flattening on the surface.

Where we walked lies sodden with
brown leaves, green haloes once
crowning anonymous birds . . .
the dry leaves curled, adrift
on the water—stem-scrawl,
cryptographic, disappearing.

The man has climbed the bank to the orchard.
With each spike-billed arrival
branches bend. How calm
he stands below them.
If he could hear the hearts of ravens,
think of the din.

What home? What refuge? Smoke
answering beyond the highest branch . . .
raked leaves are burning. Have patience.
The boat will come to you.
Even as we wait, look—late apples
drop like small flames.

Look far. He's entered a field, its furrows
in sunlight, its clay the source of icons.
Further, at the field's edge, a village, the green rooftop
of a belfry—a roost among the silent bells,
ravens with their lice, and winter coming
and the scarcity of scraps.

He's not so mysterious
as being here is more than you see.
After crossing the deep narrows
you'll find stones in the field,
the solitude of shapes
in a natural asylum—

then take your leave, and when
you arrive at your old address,
finding it lacking, you'll remain
as though you had never left the field
after reaching its stillness.
He'll enter the village and return

here, as you will, knife gleaming,
sharpened under an apple tree, few leaves
remaining, and having returned,
walking from the river, you'll know
in that last hour of light
what a stem writes on the surface.

The skiff slides up on the sand's edge,
but you want your books.
Lay them in the bow to balance the boat.
Take the oar. Once for always
a sparrow's song carries over water
the song upon itself.

Hear ahead. A door creates the house.

Kyiv

CLEMENCY
for Charlotte

    1.

    When, years ago,
we moved to the American Foursquare,
I cut away woodbine coiled
around a birch. Dead limbs fell.
I let a shoot grow from the bole, a sapling
now, a civil trump.

Weeds and roots cleared,
a tiger lily volunteered,
a bloom to cultivate, orange-
red petals an afterglow at dusk.

Once, early winter, you chanced on our cat—
in his mouth, blood and cardinal feathers.
You had forgotten nature's way.
Weeks later, you shouted, *Basil!*
He turned—
a bird flew from Basil's paws.

What fills in, what holds out?
Dooryard violets overrun a yard.

Sometimes I hear calls of mourning doves.
Sometimes I believe I know what compels them.

    2.

When the handsaw leapt from a birch branch,
I drew the teeth into my finger.
When I shut my eyes, branch and twigs
became a diagram deepening,
a blueprint of the season—
long, gray day, blood down the drain,

the deep stripe bandaged, pulsing.
When I knelt by a rose, I touched
black spots on the leaves, dry blood on my hand.

In turn, crows returning to the fields,
summoning crows
in the near dark, fireflies, few at first,
an early apple dropped—

white paws stalking glowed over grass.

    3.

August moves on slowly, a ripe hue
spreading from an apple stem.
Dirt deep in our lifelines,
our palms blend with the shade.
A chance-sown clemency guides our hands—strange
which flowers may survive with human care.

When I walk through Lou's garden,
Lou has worked the earth to match a vision,
shapes and depths hanging fire, or budding,
or hanging on, or dead.

Below the Carpathians,
in Lilya's fenced-in garden,
Lilya's cats and chickens
don't disturb her daffodils.
Like Lou, she knows life from life.
Her dog and goats wait at the gate.

    4.

Under the cherry tree,
nearly uprooted from spring snow,
compost becomes a black mound

of transubstantiation—
leaves layered with pitch and clay,
mixed with mulch, yield
loosestrife, mint and roses.

Wilderness is never far off.
A choice is hidden for a time,
like the maple shoot rooted
in an ostrich fern under the maple,
a sapling I let stand late one summer
years ago.
              When I lift out a shoot
I sense the fern is happy.

A crow sifts through the compost.
A mate, above, watches for something.

Seasons or the cat—
crows, you know, can count to five.

THE NIGHT OF DAYDREAM

> A place, where no place was; by nature's course
> As air from water . . .
> —JOHN DONNE

1.

I don't know how long, how far
I traveled to a garden
in the new world. Such care
they take here with so much
ruin surrounding the yard.

After the dormant
years of the old house,
the new family peeled away
the English ivy.
Peonies bud in the beds.

Buffalo, horse, Tatar,
gypsy across the lawn,
distant cousin to whelk
and auger, hunted between
the bellflower and larkspur—

where is my belly not
its own country? How
easy it is to be displaced
in such a small shell,
a mote upon the world.

Under ligularia,
the golden ray, the harvested
light, to stonecrop
I climb. I'm where I find
myself, house or grave.

2.

Robed and undecided,
I was a monk on muddy roads.
Often a holy man crossed my path.
Incarnation came at nightfall.
My trail is my own.

I've not forgotten the winter roads
or the holy man, on his back
his paints and wooden panels.
Not until now have I understood
the nourishment of a leaf.

Like a child curious about whorls,
I see myself from stalks
as if turning round a corner.
Let me have my place
in the shade among violets.

I move and hope for the gardener
with something childlike
leftover. My penance is to eat
among snakes. I think
of the pierced viper of icons.

Never before have I relished
an abbey so, mine
among sweet alyssum, the day lily,
the primrose. Oh penitent on thornapple,
on verbena nodding in the wind—

such fidelity from my door.

3.

I am a skull with its snail.
I am a shell with its brain.
I coin the world. Unfolded from silence

I enter the yard through intuition.
I slide my body like a hurt foot,
stretch out, hold on with secretions.
Behind my eyes feelers touch
topography, test the surfaces.

I commute to the dark—the rot
of a fallen birch, the covey
of stones. I pull myself up
to a hollyhock or hosta spreading.
The spiral of my shell winds left
over right, the knot never tied,
turning toward arrival, habit
of journeys, the slow push of my body.

Let me tell you the snail is not a slug.
The shell is not inhibition. Under rocks
or decaying leaves, I combine the sexes.
I lay the eggs. Each eye I pull in
at the calculations of a beak—the wren
keen as a vulture battering my shell.
I let go at will, dropping like a shoe.
I call on the craft of the room I made.

I right myself. I fold myself, always
in prostration, coming and going—
my damp sole the last to disappear.
As in drought I make a mucus pane,
a layered vision to seal the door.
Even for me, time is a maggot waiting.
I plug the door with my life.
I bury myself in winter.

    4.

After days of heat, rain
does the work of my belly,
filling the cracked clay,

cooling the nautilus cloister.
Lightning frightens the hounds
and child in their house beside the garden.

My path is pale light
after rain, under fireflies
reflected on my trail. This breeze
I know and a wing's stroke
upon stillness. I turn leaves
to stone, prisms into corridors.

Thick with residue,
I enter my dream at daybreak
on the spiral globe,
my domain. Repose
is appendage. My life fills
my shadow on the walls.

5.

My house of Scholastics admired
the diligent and dialectical
powers thought relevant
to a snail ascertaining what there is
in this world, his risks and his restlessness,
his sense of touch, an utter reticence
at displeasure, till birds
tweak out his vulnerable eyes,
then the visceral degrees of liquid.

Despite my fellow Scholastics,
no existence is a panacea.
If not a bird at dawn, I pray
a gardener find some worth—perhaps,
a streak of color on my shell—
and place me among wildflowers, safe
from diatoms and ashes—
so it is: one prayer from one
found at this plane of being.

6.

The place where you find yourself
   the place where you are found

your sudden disgust
     at the trail behind you
  at such golden imaginings
    the borders where you strayed

the birds that never miss
  a moment of your carelessness

your carelessness
  the map charted from your mistakes

    from one's own lead

7.

Death came first in a bell tower.
Death was hunger on the steppe
in a season of plague. How long
I did without I don't remember.

Sunlight was breaking on
the just-turned fields across the Styr.
Dry roads at last, the belfry
floor smeared with droppings.

The birds set out for the furrows,
gardens filled with leaves.
Days would never be the same.
Nights became miraculous hours.

8.

I ask you, Can patience be the virtue
of a snail, is virtue natural?

Can virtue be an instinct, must something
be overcome to possess a virtue—

what we call wisdom rather than impulse?
Does impulse lead to wisdom, the careful

march to a fallen mulberry? Impulse
or instinct, the desire for one more leaf,

dew covered, dazzling at sunup? One
leaf, we say, then the slow return. The nest

high up and the mama bird wakes, singing
at the arrival of breakfast across the lawn.

    9.

Once a tower, now leaf and bird,
or child with a stick,
or by the gardener's hand, death
comes as a myth you must believe:
the stray moon in the sky's reflection
when you cross the planktonic
circle of skeletons, when your cells
plug your lacerated pores.

Clouds cover the stars
in your sudden legend of summer.
Far off, silence begins
to ring as it does for the deaf,
the desperate monk—the bell rope
pulled at Sabbath-call,
the ancient clapper stolen,
melted by the blacksmith.

Like a live coal
fallen through the grate
to burning embers, you retire

to the wet heat of your room.
Your eyes turn inward,
their hot stalks entering
your melting brain, deep
in the body of night.

In the dream, the lame horse
is set free on the steppe, the snow
coming hard, the horse falling
slowly to sleep in the heavy drifts.
Then the evaporation—summer air
moves under stone arches, through the vacant
corridors of the dark abbey
fly and ant shall enter.

Coda

By the stone fence at the garden gate,
under birch shade over wild ginger,
a trail striped the leaf, a hoof's wake.

The slime path was time spared
beneath the inflorescence of columbine . . .
a millstream following its wheel,

a line, incandescent, upon the icon.

ONLY TO LISTEN

A boy half wakened
downstairs, I heard footsteps,
the banister creaking
from weight of a slow body
near the top of the stairs.

I believed sounds were explainable.
Yet the body kept climbing.
The fan spun at the ceiling
like a bird tethered
to a spindle. I sat up

and though the sounds ascended,
I could not go out to see
or call to my grandfather across the room,
or to the darkened corners
of that house. I know

that without the thrum,
the thrum filtered in from the fan
and moments
of my grandfather snoring,
I could not have stood the knowledge

no one was or could be
like the one heard on the stairs.
I had only to listen
and it was clear
how the dead sound mortal.

Sleep took me.
I woke to laughter, sunlight,
to the sounds of voices at breakfast.
I woke with a story from the dark.
I met a household of disbelief.

CARMINE STREET

1. Saturday Sunrise

A young soprano sings
scales through the bedroom wall,
open notes held, rounded,
then a soft tremolo extended,
as if singing a vowel slowly,

then she's joined
by a young man caroling
scales in a tight staccato,
by the erratic tick of steam in the pipes,
by a teakettle nearing its whistling pitch,

by the routine roar of a jet
progressing south
above low, gray clouds,
and high against them
gulls soar past the window,

and after the penultimate sip
of my last cup of coffee—
while I smoke a second bowl
of Lamplighter—comes
a moment suddenly of surfaces,

of shadows abiding and depths,
water beads fat on the kitchen sink,
a gurgle in the drain,
a limb's tap at the gray window,
church bells and the hour of setting out,

doors closing, the tumble and click
of locks, voices in the hall,
jackhammers starting up at
the Avenue of the Americas,
and higher the hum of traffic,

the horns and sirens,
where locals walking streets
of the neighborhood know
the frictions and sonorities of morning.
Soon, I'll join you.
                            Fare well!

2. Kindling Light

Past low brick buildings along Carmine's cobblestones,
past the Odessa cobbler's Magic Shoe Repair,
past Our Lady of Pompeii, once St. Benedict the Moor,
back to the red-striped awning of the Greenwich Village Bistro,
where I breathe cigarette smoke
from couples at their coffee or their afternoon's
golden light in tall glasses of beer,
back to my flat, upstairs, next door
to Poe's poor address—one-thirteen-and-a-half—
where Poe stretched out after one more brandy,
dropped his black boots and slept under pink streaks
in a peerless, blue sky darkening: Venus appears,
and the overlap of haze—the brightening
wash of the many lights reflected—pales nightfall
above Sixth Ave. Rain-thick clouds
and traces from smoke billowing somewhere near
ease in just below freezing, over the ever-twilight
near midnight, a once before and nether time
and time to come and Venus bright enough still
and what I see through this turning dark is—
in measured pace, day and night—how the city's made
and a day buried. Finally a hard rain
is upon us, upon us all, between earth
and another planet clear beyond the cloudbank,
till gone the dark, the haze and morning star
when sunlight gathers warmth in the courtyard.
A breeze ruffles the feathers of
a house sparrow lit in a locust tree.

PART II

BROOKLYN TO MENATAY

After Seventh Ave. the subway ascends
   with two stops on the wide curve crossing
the Gowanus Canal. Late sunlight
   glistens off Manhattan and the river,
my train returning underground,
   at Bergen gaining speed beside an A-train
—closer the strobe of windows, the faces
   I think I could come to know,
feeling the tension of possibility—
   sundering, descending at York,
such momentum under the floor of the river
   (an inverted suspension),
bolting through limbonic depths,
   intervals lit by bare bulbs
as if past lantern light at cabins
   on a shore of New Amsterdam,
timeless as the Lenape upriver,
   a line of canoes to bury a brave
barefoot on Menatay, with unstrung
   bow and empty quiver
as currents fuse in the third rail
   from the slow application of brakes,
sending me forward and back again
   under the vertical city I climb to—
there paused at a low ledge of clouds,
   the half moon at bay.

SHORE AND SEA

Yesterday, a man with tattooed biceps
posed for a picture in the sun. Each tattoo
was a mountain, a wave when a mountain moved,
not a symbol of anything, but an indication
nonetheless, a disposition for him,
a bristling someone for a Saturday night—
tattoos for a shy girl, one Betsy Providence,
perhaps, to smile at her name across his chest.

Far past him, from the break of waves,
worm-drilled shells were piled, a boneyard drying—
a hermit crab stared from a whelk. Years ago,
waves broke farther out, but yesterday
sea asters were building up again
their summer buds rooted in the sand
of trees. An ant scaled a sea oat swaying.
A mockingbird sang from the dunes.

My head on a pillow, I face the ceiling
and hear a low tide rise and fall,
exhaling small breaths, and hear wind
drift toward sunup through spiked palmetto,
and the beginnings of birdsong, night's
last to sing, a whippoorwill, all these sounds
imprinted—I imagine from a shore a sea,
calm as a lake at dawn and endless.

ACQUA ALTA

Pale lapis sky, gold the afternoon, a breeze
through long, cotton curtains at San Trovaso
opposite your room, Pound, 1908,
"dye-pots in the torch light," —even now
gondolas await repair at the clapboard shop,
pitch fires smoldering near the anvil.

Ever a cock crows in a village,
ever the corrosion seems irreparable,
ever the unforgivable and amends
and something coming together again—each cloud,
a tattered rocca, distills an hour and epoch
passing . . . birds mate at San Michele.

Always maneuvered by the lithe boatman
a keelless boat arrives over detritus
and stems of seagrass, green-flamed in the current,
and dusk's diagonals deepening, and a few fish
moving farther on, under the rippling of
the smooth flowing, your cadence upon it.

THE ENTREPRENEUR

began with a degree
in mechanical engineering,
selling dark laminated furniture
from the back of a rented truck.
The end of his first day out
his hand-lettered sign read CHEAP . . .
the rest of it ripped down
by an unprofitable wind.

Now he rents the store
in this little town.
The posters in the plate glass windows
advertise SALE and VALUES,
and country boys,
wearing their Sunday best,
sell his ensembles for every room,
admiring the legends of beginning.

With a modest oak desk
his office is the place
for computations, a motif
of cubes and spheres,
his little print of Kepler
for moments of inertia. And always
at the counter, someone pays
cash for half the balance.

But there are occasions,
and for these he has
his collectors, a different breed,
proud to be from the country.
At Rotary he calls them
his Gestapo. They're in
their cubicle now, sipping coffee,
enhancing the county's oral tradition,

telling the one about the divorcee
who crawled from a side window
of her house, baring her ass,
et cetera. Soon the collectors
will lick the powdered sugar
from their fingers, and load
their revolvers in accordance with
his principles of force and matter.

SEQUEL

Had Perseus scalped Medusa, that bitch,
hounds would have sprung from the sloughed-off skins
and the hero questioned his dagger, his gods
and himself at the wondrous evolution of paws,
at the large round eyes, at that head
become in his wet hands a sister,
a woman once with dogs on the brain,
and a snake become a man's best friend.

So it is for Ulysses, that snake in the grass
—only his dog knows him from his wanderings—
revealed to son, then the old woman,
then the men and his wife in that blood-soaked house.
Force is why there are so many dogs here
in the abandoned house of Franz Joseph.
They have been multiplying in all the houses
fallen from all the reigns, since Ovid died in Tomis.

A dog domesticated by scraps,
if ever wolf or fox, follows me,
its empire the length of a building.
Barking, another from an alley appears,
as if on a tether. I awoke last night
to a pack barking—a dog squealed and yelped,
hurt by someone, then the running silence
of dogs . . . their distant barking.

Today it might have been any dog with
a leg not touching the icy street
at Market Square, any dog with solemn eyes,
waiting for a hand up beside a beggar,
beside the woman selling sunflower seeds
and thick wool socks, beside the men wavering,
arguing, stammering from vodka,
or by the man who stands alone and stares.

I'd like to think it was one of the lucky ones
that waits at the door of a food shop,
is fed a pinch of cheese, or the one that finds
a patch of sunlit walk and sleeps there
beside another. I like to think of the pup
finding the woman with her round, layered cakes
and she, with her fat hand, reaching down,
tousling the damp fur, then turning back to wait.

But who when the villagers were returning
to villages, with onions and potatoes
turning soft, sprouting in their heavy sacks, who
was the tall woman in fur coat and hat, who paused
at the closed doors of the church, who bowed quickly
and crossed herself and dropped a few kopeks
in the hand of a cripple, and a few feet farther
knelt to the dog sitting on the walk?

She touched its head, gave it a link of sausage
good enough for anyone's pot and at the sound
a dog makes through gnashing teeth, when it lunges
at another, she didn't break stride—the fight
struck in the near dark from a coil of hunger,
like a small fire in air over a patch of snow,
the whirling smoke, and in moments
the burnt one slithering away.

Chernivtsi

THE INCORPORATION

Below the Fourdriniers,
reading gauges on steaming pipes,
filling stainless steel cups with pulp to test and record,
I was citizen of what I saw.
Where molding met at a corner of the floor
I was a shadow cast
by a bare bulb
burning without a light switch.

Upstairs,
my scream for the hell of it yawned a silent O
at the shrieking machines,
each a city block long.

I tried to decipher
what seemed a secret kept by that fraternal noise
or by the hands of millwrights
never to shape the alphabet
of their knowing—the palindrome
of indelible hours—
digits given up to the woodchipper's blades.

I followed a rat to the wharf,
to smells of creosote, salt air and sulfite,
to the corrugated night,
heavy still with heat of the afternoon;
arc lights above the pier
cast no shadow darker than
the mill's above the water—
those mirrored lights rising between mill bank and marsh.

Smoke funneling across the constellations
set the moon in motion—
the dark extending north across the Savannah,
to clear stars at the horizon's black margin.

I knew if I was not at the edge of it
or it was not something in me,
I would be lost and the mill become the world at large.

So soundless the stillness around the rusted cranes,
I wondered what made
the moon outweigh the sun at daybreak,
while the rank mist speckled my face.

TRIBUTARY

> *in memory of Malcolm Cowley*

In Savannah, the day you spoke
at our college symposium,
you were seventy-seven, the one exile left,
your cheeks a blush of broken veins,
tributaries found on a map of the Juniata.
You lectured on Aiken, our native son,
"Who acquired a reputation," you said, "without
being caught in the act, as if by a product
of auto-osmosis." *Maître*, Faulkner called you.

You talked of Scott, Hart and Brother Bill.
You saw them, not us, when you fielded
departmental queries, tempering Freud's
influence on the Lost Generation. You thought
the Love Generation had communal leanings,
against private accomplishment.

March twenty-first—about to graduate,
I was the age of Fitzgerald
when he published *This Side of Paradise*.
Camellias and dogwood had blossomed.
The ocean lapped the coast
like a lakefront tide. We gathered for seafood
at a franchise restaurant. Your red tie
and suspenders matched your plaid jacket.
A gold watch chain linked your pocket to your lapel.

"I don't recall how much German beer
we drank at the Hotel Tourain in Boston,"
you said of your first meeting with Aiken.
"I was a Junior, and editor of *The Advocate*—
he told me to look for his orange tie
brighter than his Valencia hair."

Then the young professor told his story: Crane,
drunk on the ledge of a second-floor window—
a woman acquaintance shouted, "*Jump,
Hart, you'll hurt yourself!*"
You'd had enough of suicides, you answered,
shifting table talk to agrarians,
"We'll turn asphalt, spreading like locusts,
back to petroleum, uprooting
the green cambric handkerchiefs of lawn."

Years later, snow covers the ground
where I live now in central Pennsylvania,
what Faulkner might've called
nature's travail. "Dear Jesus, this inchmeal
business of dying," Aiken wrote you.
And not that I knew you, Cowley,
yet that I might write as you near the end—
"I really was," and with confidence,
"I am and was this."

RITSOS

They wonder how I keep going—
they whisper, "Delusion,"

not knowing I transfer
day after day, from pocket to pocket,

the glass eyes taken
from the ashes of the wooden horse.

COMING DOWN

High up a crow flying fast
over the Village, over
a starling resting on a TV aerial,
then with enough thrust
to set the aerial shaking
the starling shoves off,
flying fast over the Village.

I'm following
a lean, gray-haired man
walking north, who stops
as at a riverbank.
He looks across Seventh Ave.,
at St. Vincent's
and makes the sign of the cross.

Late afternoon—in apparent stillness
dark clouds coming in,
the wind picking up—a cold drizzle
comes. Sparrows disperse
like a handful of postcards
tossed up at the so what,
coming down wherever.

TURNING FIFTY, MID APRIL

When the purplish-pink flowers
of an old redbud tree
give way to stems, their leaves
sprouting heart-shaped and dull green,
already darkening,

new shades of green are repeated,
the varying shades
of maple, apple, Russian olive
and the dogwood too in transition
between flower and leaf

despite the universal
blight of my region.

STANDARD TIME

Quartered deadfall from the hills, oak cut
to length, fresh still the smell of woodgrain,
a cord to heft, to calibrate angle and curve,
to fit, to balance high the stack
in rootless equilibrium.

As if to make a windbreak, stone on stone,
beside a mound of leaves—each leaf from its birth
notch to the black meld of compost—
I build on the birch I cut
and parceled last summer

and on the apple limbs trimmed,
their evenly spaced
woodpecker's chiseled wells—
instinct's measured patience,
the belly's need.

Migrant, flocking in, or piling up,
clouds west of here, gray on gray
arrive from the sky pyre
dying out—the sky a vault now,
a stone basin overturned.

Back again, yesterday's rain
to freeze, to splinter,
to rot what is, comes slowly on
the wind above the chill stillness.
The stack is made,

the tarp spread over for the rain,
for snow on this starless night at this return
to Standard Time, years of sap-driven life to burn,
to keep a self warm, to sleep awhile
down through ages of root and stone.

AFTERNOONS INTO EVENINGS
for my mother

1. *North*

Late June, gray with the last of daylight
we sometimes see in dreams,

then a streetlight on at the corner—
blocks away, a dog barking.

A bird by the porch repeats a dry
chip note.

There is a breeze though the leaves do not move.
You nap, puffing breaths, in a wicker chair.

From the table
the candle's shadow stretches on the wall.

How quiet evening becomes . . .
children's voices, far off,

and thwacks, just audible
down at the municipal tennis courts.

Nearby, an air-conditioner kicks on,
rattling its casing.

Somewhere a door slams.

Beside you, our dog sits panting . . .

the wind chimes
motionless as stalactites.

2. Greenville, Alabama

The only picture saved from the house fire,
a pink-tinted print of you at three—
a large Easter bow, its tight knot
pinned to your bobbed hair, your thick bangs
a dark ridge above your brows.
The tempests to come are there.

Looking down, you guard some joy
in your right eye, the luminous side of your face,
a shadow on your left eye, a grim circle
beneath it. Your snub nose will straighten
to principle. Lips poised—this
a portrait of what is known too soon,

this first flowering, its thorns
touch must negotiate. The wide neckline ruffle of
your white dress seems a weight on your tanned shoulders.
On the photographer's backdrop,
two trees of summer—beside them
you are Marion Luke, real and out of place.

3.

Lost from you,
your body
lies facing west
and you, within
morphine's
dark current,
further out.

If you drift
back to us, toward
the pale border
of light, perhaps you hear

and hold in mind
our voices in the depths
of your deep quiet.

Mother, here
further in
from where you are
the Oriental poppies
overrunning the garden,
where you walked in sunlight,
are open wide again.

4. *Last Photograph*

From your salt and pepper hair
a gray wisp falls across your forehead, a moment
of wind in one tree and not another.

You are looking up through trifocals.
Having turned eighty-nine in spring,
you are tired, very tired.

If you could allow yourself to turn away,
you would. It is as if mist after rain at dusk
in deep summer veiled your brown eyes.

Despite the tumors crowding your brain,
your right eye brightens
(and love I think is there)

as though another answer
were possible, yet questioning what you see—
your left eye stares, heavy lidded.

How you returned after each setback,
the fruitlessness now—your thin lips straight
in the bitterness of your tenuous knowing.

Your cheek rests on your knuckles.
What you have always kept you keep.
The place in you for tears is spent.

You will turn away in silence.
Starkness demands it: the recognition of
futility against the inexorable—

that dark weight with the substance of all one's days
in a pan of the scales of consolation
weighs less than what is left to live.

5.

A July evening like winter dark rolling in . . .
I lifted you, heaving you into bed.
Your head found the pillow.

Through sleep's hidden passages
you entered the coma. In the time
you believed the world made, you did not wake.

Still your earth turned through those days.
Perhaps sunrise brightened their dark
the way the moon illumines a bare field.

Bees outside your window
gathered on the purple bee balm
swaying on the windless afternoon,

through the moment following—
I cannot conceive the way
you passed away, or else I have.

You slept a sounder sleep.
We washed your body on the bed.
We dressed you in a cotton gown.

We stood and stared.
Our grief waited for the hospice nurse
to legalize your natural state,

for the funeral men to place
your body in a green bag, zip it,
roll you out on a gurney,

then drive you off . . . the bees still
draining the blossoms—your room
an emptiness I had not known.

    6.

How simple for you
the intimate step,
the letting go, as if a blossom
had a say in its downturn.

How far away, finally, final is,
gone, simply gone,
but there will be
as long as time allows

the open window,
the temperate afternoon
in July, bees about
the just-bloomed bee balm.

Be where you wished
after fifty-one years, alone—
where your husband is,
close at hand.

It was what was left,
a presence, a trace in the air,
a way of life for you. You believed
in love's obligations.

7.

You are no longer
far south in the small house

with only months having passed
since I have seen you, or days

since a phone call, your soft timbre
of breaths from your effortful life.

A heart before the kiln remains
separate till the heart ignites.

8.

Smoke drifted from the Oakwood Crematorium—
something of you in the afternoon light.
Services to mourn will soon be done
and mourning will not.

How will it be when it can be?
Mourning is the sorrow
and in the making of a place.
Always within an instinct for a future
bees light on the blossoms.
I don't know where the hive is.

Atoms of remains fell
on shoppers at the shopping center,
on cars and pastures,
on wildflowers—a dust on the pollen
ingested in this valley of
a northern mountain range.

From heat and red clay,
to rain-driven through topsoil,
to cold clay of ancient preserve
comes your body.

9.

July, chill in the air,
bee balm just now blooming,

yet by four the afternoon
was temperate as

the day you passed away.
Birds sing the same tunes,

intermittent, unsurprised by
the answer—a sudden presence

of a like-bird perched on a close branch.
What is new is the absence,

natural as birdsong after extinction.
Alive the insistent and scattered sound,

a gathered body of cicadas,
their chant quickening,

easing into night—a breeze
moves through the wind chimes.

10. *Savannah*

Hours of my childhood,
of a hurricane's acceleration—

warmth raising sea depths,
rain and wind, headlong

then landfall the torrential lashings—
our jerrybuilt house,

hours in a room
lit by a candle,

meals you cooked
over a can of Sterno,

the storm's eye passing,
the hours of slackening weather . . .

the days
and nights of what has happened.

PART III

THE RENAISSANCE

Born from geometry
on a day we never lived,

the planes of otherness
in their light of dream,

no less real than when
we lay our heads in sleep,

in separation from our days
darkening faster into the past—

days mingled out of sight,
part of last night's dreams,

whether we remember them,
or not. We add them

to impossible happenings,
solutions for our days and nights,

our durations, real as they are and of
what we see, of all

we add to what we know—
our creation,

this sudden day.

ISLANDERS

for Robin Becker and in memory of
Sarah Bowman and Eleanor Haasis

1.

Not till I saw the blue trim and cedar shingles
   did I know what a Cape Cod was.
Dolphin Head was Eleanor's—over the mantle
   a watercolor map of Edisto,
a carved dolphin over the hearth. Plump, short
   "aunt" Eleanor was the sun's warmth.
Sarah, cropped hair, square-chinned, rangy,
   a taciturn biologist we called
Bluebird, made the repairs.
   They're old-maid companions,
Mother said, sincerely. With sunlight
   mirrored late in a long mirage,
Bluebird took the seine
   and me with a bucket for seawater
down to a low tide to find
   specimens for her porch aquarium.
Bluebird on the beach held one of the poles.
   Light shimmered in the steepening
crests of waves, translucent greens folding
   to white spray collapsing
to swash and backwash. Circling,
   I brought the seine to shore.
Our slackened net lay in the shallows.
   You'll feel as if you're meeting friends,
Bluebird said, *when you call them by name.*
   She pointed how what seems near may be deeper
and into light *coral branch, wentletrap,*
   moon snail, coquinas—some with open shells,
like butterflies. What was left
   was taken by waves, so much
already in the tank. Her mail-ordered seahorse
   and mate maintained their dignity

upright in the glass habitat. I
   didn't see the male give birth—
the aquarium covered for the night,
   a towel for the magic dawn.

2.

        A table lamp on
and the yellow radiance from the dial
   on the bakelite radio, signals in
far from Dolphin Head, time
    and tidal subtractions in the moon's orbit—
      shadows through wind off water,
shadows from two winters in the mind's eye. . . .

I walked with Bluebird to the ocean's edge.
   Phosphorescence trembled at our feet
and I knew from summer that even in the dark
   waves sort creatures and things—
how wave-jostled and sand-ground,
   stones are separated, silt worn
into surfaces, how storms erase a beach,
   how beyond the rows of bunched reeds
at daybreak, loose sand records what touches: footprints
   or rain-prints, scars from the lightest of debris. . . .

Darker the winter nights in Savannah,
   weeks after I was born—my father
in a hospital, Mother at his bedside,
   and Bluebird come down to my crib.
What songs for severance did Bluebird sing?
   I'm listening. I can almost hear
her voice and the voice of him I saw
   and can't remember—near
receptions through time's static,
   wind in the hollow of a whelk.

3.

Summer again. A big-eyed boy, I awoke
   wiping sleep's crystals from my eyes.
I was safe in the salt air and smell of coffee
   percolating. Sounds from night I could see
in their making—the waves' small roar at arrival,
   palmetto fronds tapping the window trim,
blue to shield against the island dead
   able to assume the shapes of creatures.
Soon I was barefoot on the porch,
   Bluebird's whelks and conchs arranged on the sills,

and Eleanor saying I was just in time
   as a trawler passed, dragging its nets.
Her demitasse placed on the table,
   she called out, *Porpei! Porpei!* to the waves,
and the backs of porpoises, like stones
   oblong and dew-covered at sunrise, began to weave
their wake—light from depths offered up
   to morning, inroads blazed and sunken.

DEMOPOLIS

Grandmother's yard was a shadow
drawn wide under the trees,
the well an ancient window boarded
and I pushing a pecan between timbers,
listening. An eye pressed to a gap,
I could not see the dark surface.
Dusk recovered the tremulous
hymn of locusts, rising and falling.
Then lamplight, then late,
Grandmother in a cotton gown
sat looking into her mirror,
her hair let down to her shoulders.
Her brush stroke entered as if through water,
each return a mute circle,
a law of motion,
as I stood watching from another room.

STRANGE COMING NEAR

It is Monday, February fourth,
the hour before nightfall,
snow wind-whirled in the bay thickets,
in the light sway of bare trees.
A pine creaks about to snap.

Not far off, an eagle's high-pitched staccato cry
at what is strange coming near.
The gray sky darkens, at times a bit of blue,
and among the clam shells and rusting cans
the low lake filling, nearly frozen.

I am undone gradually, taken in
as part of something. Call it
the woods' mood, a burnt ascent
offered to the leaf falling.
Leaves, reeds, small twigs

and strips of bark lie encrypted
in the slow thaw as if on bleached parchment
fading, these pieces of other seasons
read like remains of a meadowlark,
a sense in kind, in the cold moment.

STRAY STONE

Each glance, the play of winter light on woods—
a camera's useless for the exactness

of each thing seen to be remembered,
a steep slope, late afternoon,

thorn and bramble thickets where the hill
drops off at what must've been the cellar

wall from this stone foundation, this
dirt pit of stray stones, the deer,

its profile resting on a stone,
its legs open, its ribcage an empty lodge

of thin fur—the rest picked clean
by whatever picks clean in a forest—

its face not belonging to the devastated,
its eye at ease through freezing nights and days

and the damp blood on what remains
glistening in the thaw.

DAYLIGHT GHOSTS

Just before nightfall, wind
arrives through tall pines, a compact roar,
a high wave breaking, the loose surf
the sound of maples, then heavy rain,

then heavier till tapering the near
darkness at my cabin door. The sun
cloud-masked, the rain passes,
far away a dog barking, barking.

A meadowlark begins its song among
the scattered overlap of last songs and sudden
sunlight cast on the stillness of puddled water,
the shagbark's dark hollow an eye toward loss.

The dog quiets and bird too—close by,
the shadows of trees, depths of silhouettes
beyond the screen of moonlight entering
the footpath entering the forest.

SOUNDINGS

in memory of Sidney Morgenbesser

Each new glimpse is determined
by many, many glimpses before.
  —WILLEM DE KOONING

  1.

Driving back again, I cross
the tidal river, sunlight studding
the bridge. Shadows over and of
the vegetation continue.

Cherokee roses and blue
hydrangeas bloom by the graves,
where a stray dog buries a bone
under the flight of a carved dove.

Here, miles I live by come to an end,
back here with the salt smell,
here in a simple place,
sunlight on a shell, the wind.

  2.

All along I've known
no breath is regained,
yet I've come back
to the chill at daybreak,
to vernal light of similar days.

Squat palmettos applaud the wind
picking up when the tide rises—
gift to barnacles on a jetty,
a columbarium, then menagerie
when the high water levels off.

3.

Gulls fly low along the shoreline.
They keep their distance,
flying again, settling behind me,
as if following the logician's
certainty, the if and only if
that never comes always,
and posted for the route I've taken:
bits of wrack, identities,
my shadow a carapace
glimmering in seafoam
clawing back over a shard of glass,
a wentletrap, and open-winged—
the coquina's unbroken hinge.

4.

Again the shorebird's
     complaint creates
  and recreates
    the shorebird's complaint.

5.

I remember an afternoon,
    an outboard droning,
  its hull slapping calm waves.
They flashed in sunlight.
    The distant boat and a few clouds
  shadowed the ocean, a weight
held down by atmosphere.
    A fisherman cast a fishhead—
  the drag clicked on his reel.
Each catch acquired a recollection
    and a moment of belief,
  like the shark's tooth I took

from debris of broken shells,
    the what it was I recalled,
  belonging more to me
than the wet sand it glittered on.
    I remember, above the tide line,
  a jellyfish crowned with flies, that lump
a silent heart, its heart a bruise.
    I watched waves comb from silence
  to silence waiting
at the future's dry mouth promise.
    Even now, fish slap
  a bucket's sides.

  6.

I walk back from where the river
meets the ocean, where I found
the mud-caked whelk,
its streaked violet shades
sanded by undertow
and the ocean's ribbed floor.

Far off, the waves
their own dark residence
began to build. Surf settled
higher with the absence of seafoam.
On the gray beach, a deadwater
more solemn than a low tide.

Then the low rumble of thunder,
the forked tail steadied
the tern's high retreat.
My shadow disappeared.
I tossed back the shell.
Mud spun from the whorl.

Waves reshuffled
the sound of wind

and gulls' cries,
each a lie and a truth,
the self's gossip, a story hued
under conditions of duress.

When the cloudbank passed,
dusk and a blue sky—
the thing by thing given up
waited: the who-I-am, worm rock,
sea whip, my shadow again
and the white skeletons of the stony corals.

7.

The porch light closer, black
the blue trim of the house.

Behind me phosphorescent water
folds over the tideland

as though a route once
of hope on a map of promise.

Morning twilight, its stars
were pale cinders, the gentle undoing

of an absence. Morning was
my horizon, my feet in the sand.

Here the stars are back now,
shining as sun-bleached shells

spilled from a croker sack.
The porch light, closer still—

flat, smack, smooth the waves sound.
Here I knew without thinking,

but not anymore as if
everything I touch hints ash.

The boardwalk rots in shadow.
Cedar shingles lie in the cockleburs.

Once, a boy here, I dreamed
sea worms covered my chin.

Now wind drives the seasalt deeper
into the soft timbers of the house.

Gone the blue, bamboo shade
at the west end of the porch—

blue paint chipped on the floor.
Windows are layered in salt.

The sea begins a hundred yards out,
deeper than night and gathering depth

like a dropped anchor. Despite
a shell held to my ear,

there is no sound to memory—
only remembrance, how-it-was-heard,

as in the museum I saw de Kooning's
Screams of Children Come from Seagulls.

Seeing it, I heard them again.

SUMMER SOLSTICE

Streetlights burn toward a brief darkness
between twilights to sunrise in Helsinki.
Harbor to gulf to sea, the passage now
past midnight—a black-back gull's laughing
in light wind and cold rain,

a sky like the sea seen from an airliner,
its shadow passing over shorelines . . . Was it
a rose finch lighting among chestnut blossoms,
or artic tern completing the longest migration,
or a plane, someone thought, looking up?

I'm thinking of the tern
high toward the spell of northern lights
where a fox circles, casting sparks
off the snowcrust, the fire cooling down
among birches, few in the evergreens—

the tern shadowing ax of antler,
net of willow bast, oak boat
or sewn boat, stones in the hull
to sink in shoal waters, or votive boat
in an earth-mound, an anchorage,

the carved figurehead of a creature,
theme for the journey suspended
in darkness, as at a window,
a silence. Gulls soar, for them no need
of hourglass, lead line, compass.

A ferry horn blasts through stippled light,
where the mute swan's been plying weeks alone
at the mouth of the north harbor.
I'm wondering was it a reed bunting
in the apple tree in rain, in Tammisaari,

yet I know, here, on Katajanokka,
barnacle geese pause in the harborside park—
the current rippling like a thick hide
on a slow animal disappearing at the Baltic—
troughed minutely under a blue, pastel sky—

far to the sparrow at the café table
in Tallinn, out there, where a gull rests
on a floating branch, where a dolphin
rises to rain, as to an open window.
I fear my euphoria at being alive.

KIERKEGAARD RETURNS TO A PATCH OF PARTRIDGEBERRY

> where nothing is identical to itself
> —LÁSZLÓ KRASZNAHORKAI

Snowfall and my steps deepen
on the path. I might say, they lead
nowhere—just moments to decipher
at a place farther on; even returning
here, to what's familiar, I might say,
you can never step once in the same stream.

As though I were never here
and see for the first time, I remember
how oaks sprout from winter's mulch,
how, after centuries, trees are stones
lifted by snowmelt and sunlight to shadows
of a few leaves, wind-struck like tortured things.

The stream—ice spreading from its banks—
rushes on, filling a lake, half-filled . . .
the only water here last summer
transcribed its course through reeds.
Its headway will follow again
a deep channel when the lake fills.

Sunlight angles through the pines,
their tall shadows a caped light
rippling on the lake. In the sedge
a thrush gone as if wind moved a branch
in that instant and this, in each shift
in the canopy a fresh appearance of things.

The green brightness of partridgeberry
winds among pine needles, *leaves*, woodscraps
moss-stained and streaked with rot's slow ash.

Red berries dot the frost between blowdown,
blight and deadfall below the bare-limbed
rattle and spent tents of caterpillars.

From lichen on root and stump, from sapwood
in a nurse log for a time to come, or seed,
bird-shat, a hemlock grows from a deposit of thickets.
From years I've lived, their route to here,
my overlay of days to this gray light,
my breaths—each a drawn finality

from the woods' release, to chrysaline silence.

THE VISIT

March, ice entombs the town, the smells of earth.
A clock ticks over sounds of the evening fire.

The last time on your way here, far off,
you seemed like something glimpsed,

a chanterelle from the door, what time let through.
Rain had left snow on roadsides under poplars—

greenfinch and hedgesparrow, their rattling notes
questioning above a first crocus,

and when those calls revisiting remained
over the field on that March evening

stars appeared as so many caps and stems.
Tonight you return from far away.

I step outside to greet you. We have
our memories of snow and dust,

of too long with no place to share
a trace of heat across a page.

Stalk still, you have circled north
in touch with decaying things

needing a voice. For centuries you have come
to the living as you have kept

a few of the dead alive. Burning cinders
and scent of cedar wheel

through this declining flurry as late clouds
open, deepening night.

SWEET MADNESS OF SONG

One thing is to darkness as another.
The sun's descent is mortal as my own
as long as I look, as true as John Clare's
lovely to view, the sun hung on nothing
through turns on the lake trail,
for him *neath the brooks willow row*
where woods prepare as then
seasons for the woods,
where piecemeal a deer's splayed body
becomes a buzzard soaring,
recovery reduced to recognition—
leaves and twigs their skeletal array
a natural script of runes
coming clear through snowmelt,
as all year earth groans
a song from oceans,
from the ground rising and falling
less than a meter, the tension of address
from each cell of things,
something coming to something, the song
migrating on seasonal winds.
I stand at nightfall, a common relation
at the lakeshore and as if to hear
think of silence breathing,
earth's crust on its chest,
and watch the darkening
trees within the lake—
The moons image too, John Clare said.

THE SONG OF THE EASTERN MEADOWLARK

Yellow moon in the west
and a planet
bright as a sister moon,
and thunder restless in arrival spreads,

deepens before fading, its return
an overlap of rolls and pounding—
strobes of lightning miles away
illuminating the trees' June shapes,

lit fragments of a memory
like trees retrieved
from floodwater to moonlight,
swept under by the current.

Rain, drop by drop,
accelerating through the leaves,
across gravel and stones,
passes into a long silence,

then back the moon and planet,
their orbits around our star
and earth's great shoulder turning
as if for us to find sleep,

where emptiness precedes the dream—
a patch of meadow in the overcast,
a place of self-possession—then further in,
the ongoing from the trance of days:

a bird sings beside the woods
a song apart, a bell ringing in a distant
arch overlooking a hill, limitless
the vanishing points in setting out—

the light ancient as morning light,
always its singularities,
their sorrows of a time alive
infiltrating, moving among shadows.

Here, the correspondences—
forests of Tuscan oak, chestnut and juniper,
and the maples and hemlocks of the Alleghenies,
and the down-home live oak, loblolly

pine and dogwood and a lark singing
and you barefoot, standing in the celestial
solitude of your identities—all around you
silence has sung light into song.

Notes

"Homage to Piero della Francesca": *Piero della Francesca: A Mathematician's Art*, by J. V. Field (Yale University Press, 2005).

"The mediaeval artist, working from *exemplum* rather than from life, had to come to terms primarily with tradition and only secondarily with reality. Between him and reality there hung a curtain, as it were, upon which previous generations had outlined the forms of people and animals, buildings and plants—a curtain that could be lifted now and then but could not be removed. Hence, in the Middle Ages the direct observation of reality was normally limited to details, supplementing rather than supplanting the use of traditional schemes. The Renaissance, however, proclaimed 'experience,' *la bona sperienza*, as the root of art: each artist was expected to confront reality 'without preconceptions' and to master it—in every work anew—of his own accord. The decisive innovation of *focused perspective* epitomizes a situation which focused perspective itself had helped to bring about and to perpetuate: a situation in which the work of art had become a segment of the universe as it is observed—by a particular person from a particular point of view at a particular moment. 'The first is the eye that sees; the second, the object seen; the third, the distance between the one and the other,' says Dürer after Piero della Francesca."
    —Erwin Panofsky, *Meaning in the Visual Arts*
    (Doubleday Anchor Books, 1955).

"The Magic Gardener": "An Old Cracked Tune," *The Collected Poems of Stanley Kunitz* (Norton, 2000); "Archaic Torso of Apollo," *The Selected Poetry of Rainer Maria Rilke*, translated by Stephen Mitchell (Random House, 1982).

"Map": *Art in the Light of Conscience*, by Marina Tsvetaeva, translated by Angela Livingstone (Harvard University Press, 1992).

"Kierkegaard Returns to a Patch of Partridgeberry": *Fear and Trembling*, by Søren Kierkegaard, translated by Walter Lowrie (Princeton University Press, 1974).

"Sweet Madness of Song": "Recollections after an Evening Walk," *John Clare*, edited by Eric Robinson and David Powell (Oxford University Press, 1984).

www.ingramcontent.com/pod-product-compliance
Lightning Source LLC
Chambersburg PA
CBHW030122170426
43198CB00009B/709